The Body Talks

A Journey to Discovery

Stella Santina

Disclaimer

The content and information contained in "The Body Talks" are for general guidance. The author Stella Santina has narrated her personal experiences in this book in coping with cancer and how she recovered from it. Several parts of the content and information contained in this book have been compiled from online websites and offline sources. These parts of information have been taken in good faith and believed to be reliable according to the author's best of knowledge. However, the author doesn't endorse any of the websites or other information sources in any way. The sources of referenced information could change in the future. The author cannot guarantee the validity and accuracy of the sources which may be changed, modified, or removed and thus, disclaims herself from any such changes, modifications, and removals. The names in this book have been changed to protect the privacy of individuals. The information provided in this document must not be taken as an alternative to any advice by a doctor, physician, or medical professional. The readers should not use the information given in this book for diagnosing an illness or other health-related problems. Further, the readers also should not discontinue professional medical or healthcare advice because of something they have read in this book. The content and information provided in this book does not create a doctor-patient relationship between you and the author of this book. Any reliance you make on any information presented in this book is at your sole discretion and risk. The reader agrees to hold harmless the author from and against any damages, lawsuits, costs, expenses including any legal fees, medical fees, or insurance fees resulting from the application of any of the information provided by this book.

Cover design: Stella Santina

This book is dedicated with love, hope and prayers to those battling cancer, and anyone who is struggling with life's hurdles.

Contents

Introduction

I have written this book with the hope of helping others who are on a similar journey, a journey of misinterperating life's hurdles. I have come to the realisation that when something bad happens to us, it is merely a way for us to awaken. Our body is giving us a nudge. A nudge from a Higher Power, that perhaps illness or suffering is a way for us to wake up and see what this Higher Power is really trying to show us. For myself, cancer was the wakeup call I needed, to awaken what was already within, that which is embedded in our subconscious minds. It's just remembering it. Remembering who we really are, how beautifully we were created and the power we hold within us to heal our own bodies and then go on to help others do the same. Taking care and giving love to our mind, body and soul. From the day we are born, throughout our school years, our work life and our careers, we are told what to think, what to believe, what we should learn and how we should be. We are separated by colour, race, religion, beliefs, class, education and wealth. We have learnt to judge and live separately from our fellow humans. I'm guilty of it too. I once asked my nephew when he was four years old if he was an English man, or a Cypriot man and he answered me so perfectly, "No Bebbi, I'm none. I'm not an English man or a Cypriot man, I'm a human." Sometimes we need a reality check from children. They haven't yet been brainwashed by the outside world and still see life as it should be, through eyes of innocence. After all, we have all come from the same place, we have all entered this world the same way. We were all created with the same organs, the same body parts, a heart and a soul. Why do we then create a divide between us when we are all conceived by the same creator. One day something will awaken within you and cause you to remember everything that you have forgotten. You will find who **you** really are, not who you have been taught to be and the road to awakening and rediscovery will be the start of a beautiful journey, a journey to reconnect you with your inner self.

The education system has been created to programme children to go down the same path, follow the same protocols and do well at school so they can get a good job and become "successful." Why are we not taught life lessons, the power of the human mind and how to think independently? How about we teach children that within each and every one of them, they have their own uniqueness, their own strengths, their own special qualities that they can bring forth to the world. That it doesn't matter what job they do, but more importantly the qualities that lie within them. The potential that lies within them, to love the qualities and parts of who they really are so they can help themselves to learn, grow, heal and evolve, and in turn do the same for their fellow humans throughout their lifetime. Let's teach them about the power of the Universe, the power of prayer, the power of meditation. That love is the driving force of this Earth that can help us all live more united and peacefully.

Every single one of us has great abilities, a power within us that we are not taught about, it's all about rediscovering it and believing in it. Life doesn't have to be a difficult path of survival if we just learn to open our hearts. When we discover that happiness and joy are found within us, we can unlock the secrets of our souls, and have the ability to live in a much happier, peaceful way, that requires a lot less effort than suffering and struggling to survive.

Everything is energy, everything. Whatever it is that you are feeling, you will attract. If you are feeling a lack of something or that you are hard done by and that "bad" things always happen to you, that is what you will manifest... Your thoughts create your reality. Elevate your emotions to attract good, love and abundance into your life. Feel gratitude for the little things and you will see that they will become the big things. The greatest thing I ever did, was when I started asking what each painful experience was trying to teach me. Not feeling sorry for myself or asking why this is happening to me, but instead looking for what the experience was trying to teach me. It changed everything. Try not to listen to your mind so much, rather, feel what it is your heart and soul are trying to tell you. Your mind will try to confuse you, it will make you question things, it's part of the egoic mind that we have to learn to tame. Your heart and soul know only love. They know the way. Listen in more and tune into your body. It will always talk to you, if you can just quiet the mind.

Chapter 1

Life as I Knew it

I have been putting off writing this book for the past three years. Three years of, "Not right now," but each time that voice within spoke to me. I don't know why I kept putting it off. Maybe not wanting to relive that time of my life again, or maybe the fear of being judged, but I kept hearing it: "There's nothing to be afraid of, share your story, you want to help others, don't you? Share your love." I didn't know if it was my inner voice, my soul talking to me, or God talking to my soul. But nonetheless, I felt ready to share my story, my journey, the things I'd learnt along the way, in the hope that I could help others. My journey and recovery from cancer, which I see as my gift from God.

Healing doesn't just mean to heal physical ailments or illnesses. Healing requires us to go deep within our souls and heal any emotional wounds we may have, as well as physical. Every hurt or trauma we've experienced as a child stays with us right through to adulthood. The way I see it, our souls are filled with tiny holes of past experiences that have hurt us, such as being shamed or belittled, but when we heal that part of us and learn to love ourselves the same way we would a child, we close up each hole that is seeping out pain. We fill it back up with love and heal that wound, which in turn makes us more complete and full of self-love to share with others. How can we offer love and care to others if we still have unresolved issues of our own that we haven't dealt with yet? It would be like offering someone a cupcake with bites taken out of it. Healing is not pretty or easy, reliving old memories can be a painful experience, but when you come through to the other side, it's a truly beautiful feeling that makes all the pain worth it.

Yes, the past can hurt you, but it can't hurt you twice. It's in the past for a reason, to learn, to grow, to move higher as we evolve through the lessons of life. To share your knowledge that each experience teaches. To share love in the hope of helping our fellow humans. With the power of love spreading throughout humanity, greatness can be achieved. After all, love is the highest frequency. Love always wins and the world needs more love, right?

It doesn't really matter what each of us believes, what colour we are, where in the world we are from, male or female; when you are in a place of having no control over your body, you realise you are not just your physical body. There is a greatness within and that greatness connects each and every one of us through the power of love. You are a divine being and when you allow the inner to guide you, you suddenly realise the utmost power that our souls and inner bodies possess. The higher power is within you the whole time, guiding you every day, keeping you alive. If we surrender to the noise of the world, we realise just how blessed we truly are. That every night when we close our eyes and forget about controlling our daily lives, our inner being is doing all the work to keep us alive, night, and day.

"The moment you start acting like life is a blessing, it starts feeling like one." Unknown [41]

We were created in the most perfect way. If we just trust and allow ourselves to be. We are not just a physical body, we are a divine creation with blessings all around. Through great surrender we can experience God's peace.

When I was twenty-six years old, I decided to move from England to the beautiful island of Cyprus, from where my family originated. After two years of living in Cyprus, I was beyond happy with my new life. I had recently ended a nine-year relationship which had been up and down at times. Although I felt awful for making that decision, I couldn't live with the resentment that had been building up inside of me and decided I couldn't go on living this way, it wasn't fair for either of us. The moment I made the decision, after months of putting it off, I felt a massive sense of relief; like I had been holding onto something I shouldn't have for too long. I hold no ill feelings or negativity toward my ex-partner, nor do I regret that experience in my life. There was still a lot of love shared, but sometimes, two people just don't go together the way coffee and donuts do! The only way you will find out is through experience. Life is meant to teach us. I was grateful for this part of my life and what it had taught me, but I was also grateful I had a new start, with just my self. I was embarking on a new chapter in my life. Little did I know how much it would change my life.

Chapter 2

The Dreaded Cough

Life was good. I moved into an apartment by myself and bought myself a little car. I loved my job, well more so the people I worked with, which was the start of beautiful friendships. I started going to Zumba twice a week, having coffee and dinner with friends, and was out having fun at weekends. The stress of the past was behind me and I felt good. Okay, so my diet during the day at work wasn't great, I'd just munch on chocolates and biscuits throughout the day, lots of coffee and fresh fruit juices (which I thought justified me eating all the sugary things), but hey, I ate a good meal when I went home.

September 2016. Summer was slowly coming to an end and my new, fun life was still going on, but something wasn't quite right. I kept getting a niggling cough which I couldn't get rid of. I'm one of those people that rarely gets ill and I thought that it would pass, which it did, or so I thought.

By October/November, during my exercise classes I started to find it difficult to breathe. I thought it strange as I had been doing these exercise classes for a good few months and had never experienced this before. A few weeks passed and I was still struggling with my breathing, then the cough returned. Oh man not again I thought. This time it was chestier, so I decided to try a cough syrup. After a few days, the cough hadn't shifted so I thought to try a different one, so back to the pharmacy I went. A few days later, still no change. My friend recommended I go with her to see her doctor, so I agreed. He checked me thoroughly and assumed it was bronchitis. He prescribed me antibiotics and a course of two other cough syrups and off I went.

December. After taking a course of antibiotics and an assortment of cough syrups that I had gathered at my work desk (I now had a candy shop and a pharmacy at my desk), it just wasn't shifting. It had eased off slightly but still was lingering, some days worse than others. I was planning on going to England for the Christmas holidays and thought that if I didn't feel any better when I was back in the UK, I would see a doctor there too.

I flew in to London and stayed with my brother for a night before we both headed down to our family home. We walked around London for hours. I was absolutely exhausted and all the walking felt like it was breaking me down. I wanted to just fall into bed and stay there. How could I have possibly become so unfit when I exercised regularly?

The following day we took the train to our home town. My brother and I walked the ten minute journey from the station to our brother's barber shop. By the time we arrived there, I felt like I wanted to just collapse on the floor. I could just about breathe and the cough had somehow got worse overnight. I could not understand what was going on. I had seen a cough syrup advertised on the tv specifically for bronchitis called 'Broncho Stop'. I thought that one would do the trick.

Whilst in the UK, I got a whole lot worse. My cough worsened, I had no energy, I wanted to sleep all the time and I was having awful night sweats. One day I was lying on the sofa at my mum's house, coughing as usual, and my brother said to me, "Stel, you still have this cough, you've had it since September. Go back to a doctor!" I guess he was right. I ended up going to the doctor a few days before I was due to fly back to Cyprus. She made me feel rather silly for going to see her for 'just a cough,' as she put it. "But I've had it since September," I told her. "That's basically four months." "You don't have a temperature so you're fine," she said to me "it will pass." "Are you not going to check anything else?" I asked. "You don't have a temperature, the cough will pass" and she sent me on my way. I left feeling really quite angry, I just wanted to know why I still had this stupid cough!

If you have the same annoying cough for any longer than two months, (as we are reminded of by public health ads!), or any kind of lingering symptoms, be sure to see your doctor and be persistent if need be. Our bodies give us warning signs when something isn't right. Your body will talk to you. It will flash warning signs the same way a car does when it realises something needs to be checked. Only you know your own body, so listen to it when it talks to you. Sometimes, even doctors can get things wrong. We're all on a journey of learning together.

By the time I arrived back in Cyprus, I felt like a zombie. I felt like I'd gone to sleep one day and woken up as something else. I don't know if flying made things worse due to the pressure but what I did know was that I was not myself. People would stare at me when I coughed, it was as though I was going to cough my lungs up out of my mouth. I had eczema all over my body, I was losing weight fast, I couldn't walk two steps without struggling for breath, let alone climb the four flights of steps in my apartment block which I would normally have run up. The night sweats had got ten times worse, I would wake up after a couple of hours drenched in sweat. I had to sleep upright to prevent coughing and make breathing slightly easier and I had constant heartburn. The veins in my neck and chest became raised and prominent with strange red marks around them. I just put it down to the strain of coughing.

I was so tired all of the time, that when i got home from work all i wanted to do was sleep. I no longer felt like going out with my friends and felt too drained to even talk to anybody. My body was screaming out to me yet I failed to listen to it. I knew something wasn't right, but I didn't think for one minute it could be anything as serious as cancer. At worst, I thought maybe I had fluid on my lungs.

Thursday 7th January 2016. I got up after another restless night which had become my new normal. I showered and got ready to go to work which, believe me, required so much effort, but I refused to give in.

On my drive to work, I felt a sharp pain jolt through my whole body which caused me to jerk. I pulled over onto the hard shoulder of the highway and doubled over in pain. It was like nothing I had ever felt before. I couldn't move. I was frozen, my head on my knees, praying for it to stop. After a few minutes it passed and I managed to sit back up again, my eyes watering from the pain. What was that? I thought to myself. What had happened to me? I sat there for another ten minutes and made sure I was okay to drive, before continuing to work.

My job required me to speak on the phone to potential University students on a daily basis. I could barely string a sentence together without having to cough or gasp for air. Even one of my students, over the phone, asked me if I was okay and suggested that maybe I ought to go home.

Later that morning, my friends at work could see I was most definitely not okay and begged me to go to the hospital to see one of the doctors there. I agreed and made my way there. I saw a lovely doctor who was such a sweet and compassionate lady. She listened to my chest, gave me some papers and asked me to go straightaway for an x-ray. By the time I left her office it was gone lunch time. I thought to myself, I'll go first thing tomorrow morning, I need to get back to work. Wow, since when did we stop giving ourselves self-care and self-love. How could I prioritise my work obligations over my well-being? If only I could go back and tell that girl a thing or two!

Chapter 3

The Big C Reveal

The next morning, I took the whole day off work, met my friend Mia and headed to the x-ray department. I hadn't mentioned anything to my family at this stage as I didn't want to worry them, just in case it was something that could be easily resolved.

I sat in the x-ray department waiting to be seen. About an hour later I had the x-ray taken and was waiting for them to give me the results so I could head home. The radiologist came out holding my x-ray and proceeded to point out a strange mass behind my lung. To me, it just looked like any other x-ray and made no visible sense at all. She explained that I would have to stay for blood tests and a CT scan. She told me to wait in another area of the hospital and someone would come over to see me and give me something I had to drink for the CT scan. By something, I mean the most vile drink I had ever tasted! It was like drinking a bottle of sambuca.

My friend Mia had called our friend Titos to give him an update on what was happening and he came to join us at the hospital. A couple of hours passed while we sat waiting for my results. I'm so thankful that I had friends there with me that day for moral support.

After about four to five hours of tests and waiting, the doctor called me into his office. He asked me to sit down and ever so calmly said, "Stella, you have cancer, your blood and scan results are not good. I cannot tell you what type of cancer it is without a biopsy, or where and if the cancer has spread, but it looks like Non-Hodgkin's lymphoma. Your scans show a large mass in the lymph gland behind your left lung and in your neck." Strangely, I felt numb, no emotions, nothing. Should I speak, should I cry, should I be angry? "Okay, thanks," I replied. "We're going to need to keep you in," he told me. "And on Monday you will start further tests and biopsies." My immediate thought was that I didn't want to stay in the hospital. If I only had the weekend to myself before I was to be kept in for who knows how long, I wanted to have a bit of freedom; to tell my family from home rather than from a hospital bed. The doctor wasn't in agreement, but after ten minutes of insisting that I would be fine, he reluctantly agreed. However, he asked me to sign a consent form to say I had refused to stay and that I was leaving of my own accord.

As my friends and I left the hospital, I could sense

their concern. I hadn't said a word and neither had they. I was in a weird kind of trance state. A part of me was relieved because I finally had an answer to what was wrong with me. As we walked to the car, I knew one of us had to say something and ease the situation. "I'm okay guys," I managed to say. "Let's go back to my house," my friend Mia said. "I'll meet you guys there, I'm going to call the others at work and let them know," Titos replied.

My friend Mia and I sat in her car, again in silence for a few minutes. Then it dawned on me, "OH, MY GOSH! How on earth am I going to tell my family!" I blurted out, with my head in my hands. How do you even begin to tell your loved ones that you have the dreaded disease that most people are afraid of even saying. I was trying to hold it together and not freak out about how and what I was going to say to my family.

We arrived back at Mia's house. I sat on the sofa with the results in my hand. I sat and stared at the x-ray image and all I could think was, how do they even read this thing? I couldn't even work out which way round it went! My thoughts started to wander. Great, now everyone's going to start treating me differently. They're going to think of me as the girl with cancer and feel sorry for me. That was the last thing I wanted.

There was a knock at the door. All my friends from work had left work early and turned up with snacks, pizza, love and laughter! It was like everything was completely normal. We laughed, talked, ate and even joked about the cancer. It made me so happy that they were treating me as "normal me." I will always be eternally grateful that I had friends like this at a time when I needed them most; they really were amazing.

That evening, I had planned to stay the night at Mia's. I went over and over in my head what I would say to my family and who I would tell first. "What do I even say?" I asked my friends. "I don't even know how to begin. Okay, it's definitely cancer right, before I start calling to tell them? Please just confirm it for me." "Yeah Stel" they answered solemnly. "Okay then, so here goes," I mumbled nervously as I walked off to the bedroom.

My aunty was the first person I was going to tell. She also lived in Cyprus and it was like having a second mum around. We are a very close-knit family and my siblings and I had always had close relationships with our aunties. This aunt had always been the strong one, she'll help me find the words to tell my parents. I dialled nervously. "Zee, I have something to tell you but please don't freak out. You know that persistent cough I've got and how I've been feeling unwell, well I went to the hospital today and they did lots of tests and checked me over, they're pretty sure it's cancer." (I thought that if I said "pretty sure" and not "it's cancer", it would sound a little better.) "What are you talking about?! How could they have tested you and in a matter of hours diagnosed you with cancer?! That's ridiculous, don't be so silly," she replied frustratedly and then hung up! Right... so that wasn't quite how I expected it to go.

I sat on the bed, dumbfounded. What do I do now, I thought? A few minutes passed and my phone rang, she was calling me back. "Okay," she said, "tell me everything, what tests did you have done, what doctor did you see and what exactly did they tell you?" I sat and calmly told her everything. "You signed a consent form to leave?! I'm coming to get you." "Oh Zee no, please. Let me just have this weekend before it all begins", I begged. She wasn't having it. "Please, you can come and get me tomorrow." I must have tugged on her heartstrings, because she reluctantly agreed to let me spend the night with my friends.

One down, now for my parents. My parents and siblings, four brothers and one sister all live in the UK. I knew telling them would be so much harder as they were a million miles away from me. I knew how helpless they would feel. I sat for five minutes, psyched myself up and then called my dad. "Hi Dad, where are you? Can you talk? It's kinda important." "Yeah, I can talk, what's up?" "Are you on your own? Are you somewhere you can sit?" I asked. "Stel, what's up?" "Well, I've been at the hospital all day and they've worked out what that cough is. They're pretty sure it's cancer. There's a mass behind my lung." "Stella, what are you talking about?! That's ridiculous. They've obviously made a mistake!" "No Dad, there's no mistake, I go back in on Monday for more tests, but don't worry I'm absolutely fine." "They've obviously got it wrong, they've made a mistake. I have to go", he replied. There it was again, I'm just going to hang up on you. Apparently, when you tell someone you have cancer, it's a done thing to just hang up! Obviously I'm joking; I can't even begin to imagine how it must feel for a parent or close family member to hear those words. I sat waiting for him to call back. It took him a while, but he did and he was in serious denial, not accepting that I had cancer. "Dad, can you tell the others. I can't bring myself to do it. And don't worry, I'm absolutely fine. I have everything under control, really, I'm okay."

Something I have realised on the journey of life is that as human beings, we struggle with acceptance. That doesn't mean it's a bad thing or wrong, but acceptance means to just allow what is, to really feel, and sometimes that can hurt, so the egoic mind goes into denial as a coping mechanism where we can bury our emotions instead of feeling the pain that arises. I've been there. We don't want to tolerate or deal with difficult situations, but really, all we are doing is covering something up with layers until one day it will break through those layers and force us to face up to whatever it is that needs to be accepted. It is only when we surrender to the acceptance that we create the room for peace and love to fill us.

> "Acceptance doesn't mean resignation; it means understanding that something is what it is and that there's got to be a way through it." Michael J Fox [45]

That evening, my mum and siblings called me. When we hear the word cancer, we automatically think of the worst. Speaking to my family members brought me so much peace. No matter how far away you are from your family and loved ones, the love can be felt in an instant. It didn't matter how far away we were, I knew I had the best army for the battle ahead. One made from love.

There was one person left I wanted to tell before I went into hospital, my cousin Alessa. We had grown up together and had gone through so many different life experiences. We were like Thelma and Louise, so I expected that this phone call was going to be a difficult one. I braced myself to make the call expecting her to hang up on me too! "Hey Alessa, I need to tell you something but please, please don't freak out. I need you to stay calm, because I'm really okay and I'm on a super calm vibe." "OMG, you're pregnant!" she screamed. I laughed. "I actually wish that was it" I said. "Well what then? I promise I won't freak out." As I told her and explained, she remained so calm. She completely kept it together. She later told me that ten minutes after we had ended our phone call she completely broke down to her husband. The fact that she kept it together whilst talking to me meant so much.

Finding out I had cancer didn't scare me, nor make me angry or upset. I was most upset about telling my family and friends, the people you love most. Cancer is a word so many people are afraid of and society has deemed it such a taboo subject. I knew instantly I wanted to change that. We shouldn't let our fears control us, especially as hope is stronger than fear. I knew that everything was going to be okay and this was an obstacle in my life that God had led me to in order to learn, grow and help others. All I knew is that I had to fight. As my dad put it, "Get ready to do ten rounds with Mike Tyson," man it felt like I did twenty.

My uncle said to me, "You're a lion, like your grandad. Now go and fight with the strength of a lion!" I knew I was in for the toughest fight of my life, but I was ready! If only I had known just how difficult this fight was going to be. I knew I had to keep a positive mind frame, as a negative mind weakens the immune system.

> *"The cells in your body react to everything that your mind says. Negativity brings down your immune system." Unknown.* [23]

Thankfully I was blessed with the support and love of my amazing family and friends to ease the pain of this journey. After all, Love wins.

Chapter 4

Veins and Biopsies

Over the weekend I went downhill rapidly. I couldn't even speak one word without gasping for air. I couldn't walk and my heart felt like it was going to burst through my chest. Now I realised why the doctor wanted to keep me in.

Monday morning came and we made our way to the hospital. Because of how rapidly I'd deteriorated, my aunty was furious with me for signing the consent form to leave. She was worried sick, while I was joking that at least I was still alive and we had made it to the hospital. She wasn't laughing.

We waited until a doctor was ready to examine me. I wasn't sure what to expect or what was even going to happen. In my ignorance, I had no idea how chemotherapy even worked. I had never been in hospital for anything serious apart from pneumonia when I was born, but obviously I don't remember that hospital experience. I was called into a room and a doctor checked me over. They attempted to take my blood and were baffled at how thin the veins in my arms were. "You had the same problem when you were a baby," my aunty said. "Your veins were barely visible. They struggled to take from the veins in your arm and they wanted to take blood from the vein in your head and your mum was freaking out." "Oh my gosh Zee, please don't give them any ideas, they'll find one in my arm eventually," I said. After a few minutes of opening and closing my fist, they managed to find a vein. "Hurray, no head vein," I joked.

"Your resting heart rate is overly fast," the doctor told me. It was reading at around 155bpm. "We're going to send you for a cardiograph," she said. Over the last couple of days I could feel how fast my heart was beating. I could feel every heart beat like the beat of a drum pounding on my chest. Strangely, everything around me seemed like it was all happening in slow motion. My heart felt like the raging sea, yet my soul felt so calm.

Later that afternoon, while I was waiting for a hospital bed, they informed me that I would have to wait a little longer as I had to be put on the high-risk ward in a private room, as I was susceptible to catching an illness or infection. My cells were already in overdrive, attempting to fight the cancer, making my immune system weaker.

Even after all this, I still don't think I had grasped

the seriousness of it. Once I was in my room, I was so happy just to be able to lie down, I just didn't have the energy for anything. My aunty stayed with me until I fell asleep.

The next day was biopsy day. In the morning the nurses came to do my morning checks. Blood pressure, heart rate and so on. "I don't think the machine is working properly, surely that can't be your resting heart rate," the nurse said. I could barely talk, but I tried to tell her that there was nothing wrong with the machine and that it really was my abnormal heartbeat. After trying three different machines, she finally accepted the readings were accurate and hurriedly went off to fetch the doctor. The doctor was a lovely, kind, young lady who fussed over me continuously to make sure I was as comfortable as possible. As they were so concerned about my heart rate I was sent back for more tests, before I went in for the biopsy. Thankfully there was no damage to my heart, so they were happy for me to carry on with the biopsy. I was put back into a wheelchair and my aunty wheeled me through the hospital to the biopsy room. Being pushed around in a wheelchair was a strange feeling. It took me back to being a child in a buggy. I felt a part of me drift back to that childlike state, but with a feeling of vulnerability.

I have to be honest, the thought of the biopsy had been freaking me out all night. I hadn't said anything to anyone, but all I kept thinking about was how they were going to poke a great big needle into a tumour, which was pressing against my lung and heart. What if they pierce the wrong part? Well there's no way of getting out of it now I thought to myself as we approached the room, so stop over-thinking and deal with it! I was back in the same room where I'd had the CT scan. I lay on the bed and looked out at my aunty through the open doors. She had a look of pure fear on her face, so I smiled and waved excitedly, as if I was about to take part in an exciting game. They closed the doors and told me they were ready to begin. "First we're going to give you some local anaesthetic, then put you through the CT machine to pinpoint the exact spot on your chest where we need to go through." As they con-trolled the machine remotely from an adjacent room, I was manoeuvred into the dome like ma-chine which felt dark and claustrophobic, but thankfully it was over after only a few minutes. They marked my chest and put me back through to double check. They weren't happy with the first marking, so I was put through the machine again. "Okay, we've got it," the doctor said. There was a lovely nurse in the room with me who stayed by my side and spoke to me throughout, to help keep me calm. "We're ready to go Stella," the doctor said. I looked at her holding the largest, thickest needle I have ever seen. I wanted to panic but thought to my-self, it will be over in a flash and anyway, where will panic get me?! "Okay," I replied nervously. The nurse squeezed my hand gently. In went the needle. Surprisingly, it wasn't as painful or as scary as I had built it up to be. "Oops", the doctor said, "Not quite the spot, we need to go in again." Are you actually kidding me! I thought to myself. Had my premonition become reality, or did I manifest it with my negative thoughts. Well, at least it wasn't as painful as I had expected it to be, so I didn't mind so much when she had to do it again. Soon it was all over and when they opened the doors my aunty was still standing there in the same place, with the same fearful look! They helped me into the wheelchair and wheeled me out to her. "It's done Zee, they went through the wrong place first of all but they got there in the end. It wasn't as bad as I had imagined it to be," I said chuckling. She looked relieved and we made our way back to my room.

They informed us that the biopsy results could take up to a week. My aunty had been in constant contact with my family back in the UK, updating them at every step. I was adamant that they didn't need to fly out as I was absolutely fine and had everything under control, even though I did not have the slightest idea about treatments, therapies or what was going to happen. In all honesty, everything started to feel like a bit of a daze. The feeling of vulnerability was coming and going. By now, I could barely look after myself and had to leave it to my family to make the decisions.

We were sitting back in my hospital room. "What would you like to eat tonight? I'm going to bring you a nice surprise," she said, "I fancy something sweet," I replied. I was craving my chocolates! If only I had known back then the dangers of sugar and its effects on cancer. "Okay," my aunty said. "I have to go and sort some things out and I'll be back later, in the evening. "You'll be okay, right?" "Of course," I replied. "I have my Fun Box and the DVD player." My friends from work had made me a box full of games, quizzes, letters and other bits to keep me entertained during my hospital stay. My friend Faidra had lent me her portable DVD player and the Harry Potter film collection. I hadn't watched all the films so Harry Potter became my saving grace and new obsession that kept me going through the hospital days. It was a good distraction. The love from others can be shared in so many thoughtful and beautiful ways.

Later on, when my aunty returned, I thought that she was acting strange, smirking and holding her phone up towards me. She sat down beside me, still pointing her phone at me, staring and smiling. What on earth has gotten into her, I was thinking. Maybe the stress of it all has got too much and it's driving her a little crazy! Then she glanced at the door and my dad and one of my brothers walked in! They rushed over to me and hugged me tightly. I was overcome with emotion and I sobbed and sobbed. My eyes are full and I am filled with emotion, even now, as I write this. I can't even put into words the emotions and feelings I felt in that moment. I couldn't believe that they had dropped everything and in a matter of days had flown to be by my side. "Nice surprise huh!" my aunty said.

The next few days were spent in the comfort of having family next to me. In all honesty, those days are a bit of a blur. I don't remember much and I was struggling to tell the rest of my family and friends that I was being treated in hospital for cancer... so I left my dad to do most of the telling. I had constant visits and love from my cousins and friends. My family and friends back in the UK were just as amazing. Even being so far away, they made sure their love and care was powerfully felt.

The following day, they informed me that I was going to be moved to a different hospital and that I would be taken there in an ambulance. I was quite excited, I had never ridden in an ambulance before! I asked if my brother could ride with me, but unfortunately, I wasn't allowed any guests. So my brother, dad and aunty made their own way and met me there.

At the hospital I was taken straight to the haematology department where I met my doctor. He was such a kind, softly spoken man, I instantly felt calm. There was a group of doctors and nurses in the room there with me, all talking, discussing me and my situation. One of the doctors turned, looked at me, and as if it was a completely normal thing to do, she grabbed my ponytail and said, "You might want to cut this off, it's going to fall out in a few weeks anyway." What?! I thought, how rude! Why would she be so mean and inconsiderate. I said nothing. I looked at my doctor and he smiled gently with his kind eyes. "Come on," he said "we have to do some tests." I got up out of the wheelchair and followed him and the nurse into the next room, still not saying a word. "If you lie down on the bed there, on your left side. We're going to do a bone marrow biopsy." I had no idea what a bone marrow biopsy was, which was probably a good thing, because if I had known, I probably would have tried to run to escape!

The next ten minutes were the most painful ten minutes I had ever felt in my life. The doctor stuck the giant needle into my hip and turned it again and again, like a corkscrew. I was given anaesthetic to numb the skin but NOTHING numbs the pain from your bones. It felt as though he was trying to twist a screw into my hip. I felt every turn of the needle going deeper into my bone. My leg jerked and tensed, which caused my whole body to tense up. "We're nearly done, you're doing great, just relax for me," the doctor said. All I could think of was how on earth do children go through this. I couldn't stand the pain. How do children cope! What an unpleasant experience; the thought still sends chills through me.

Later that evening my brother came and sat on the bed next to me. I was struggling to brush my hair; he took the brush from me, "Here let me plait your hair for you." I sat there while my little brother brushed and plaited my hair for me. Even now, I get tearful and my heart fills with love at the memory of this moment. Such a small gesture that can mean so much to someone who may be suffering. Love and kindness can go a long way.

The following day, Saturday the sixteenth January 2016, I was due to be introduced to the dreaded chemo. I was still none the wiser.

Over five days, I'd had two biopsies, CT scans, x-rays, cardiographs, blood tests and a team of medics constantly watching over me. The doctors and nurses had all been brilliant. I had been diagnosed with Non-Hodgkin lymphoma and the tumour was growing in the lymph gland behind my left lung, (hence the reason why I was struggling to breathe.) My doctor told me that I had to start chemotherapy immediately; six nine hour sessions, every three weeks, followed by a month of radiotherapy, Monday to Friday. I was also put on medication including blood thinners and steroids, and for ten days after chemo, I was not allowed any salt or sugar. Still utterly oblivious in my ignorance as to how chemo worked, I asked my ever so important questions:

1. Can I go to work on Monday?

2. When exactly will my hair fall out?

3. When can I eat chocolate again?

I looked over to my cousin who was sitting next to me and she looked at me as if to say, seriously, those are your questions?! Thankfully, one of us had our head screwed on and she proceeded to ask the actual important questions. Later that day, I was to begin my first chemotherapy session.

Chapter 5

The Life of Chemo

As they were looking for a vein in my arm to hook me up to the chemo drip, I had no idea this is how it worked. I had to sit for nine hours at a time while poison was pumped through my blood. The doctors were not even sure if chemo would be the cure, but they were hopeful. Who even wants chemo? I certainly didn't. Especially after reading that chemo was first developed during World War 1 as a chemical weapon! [1] Unfortunately, the tumour was growing rapidly and was now the size of two fists put together and pressing against my heart and lung, so they had to act quickly to relieve the pressure. My family wanted to do whatever was necessary to shrink the tumour, as soon as possible, so under the circumstances I didn't have much choice; it was all systems go.

The question arose of how, why and what caused the cancer. My mum had been diagnosed with Hodgkin's lymphoma at fifteen years old, so they assumed it could be down to genetics. I wasn't convinced it was that; I put it down to stress and bad diet (replacing meals with sweets and chocolates). Also, my hormones were all over the place as I had been on contraception for around ten years continuous. The first doctor I saw, explained to me that the contraception I was on, had increased the level of hormones in my body and told me that I had come off it too abruptly, instead of weaning myself off gradually; the lymph glands could not keep up with producing the same levels of hormones that my body had become used to, and he felt this could have played a part. What I have now come to realise, which I will expand on later, is the impact that negative emotions have on illness and disease. The negative emotions that we store in our subconscious mind can have an effect on the body, something that Louise Hay talks about in her book, 'You can heal your life.' (An essential read!)

My doctor explained to me that I would be attached to an IV drip for nine hours and be given a sleeping tablet so I could sleep through some of it. If I reacted well and did not experience any abnormal side effects, I would be allowed home on the Sunday evening. My dad, brother, aunty and cousin were allowed to sit with me, like guardian angels watching over me, while the chemo did its job.

I was told that the chemo would also weaken my immune system, killing off white blood cells, as well as the cancer cells, so I would not be allowed to go back to work or go out in public places. I was only allowed a limited number of visitors and definitely no-one that was sick or sniffly. I wasn't allowed to eat out anywhere in case of salmonella, food poisoning or any other infection risks, so basically I was housebound. Ironically, as I write this, we are currently going through the coronavirus pandemic and most of the whole world is housebound, in lockdown, so I've had good practise for this.

When I did go out anywhere, I had to wear a mask due to having a very weak immune system. I was not allowed to be on my own so I had to temporarily move in with my aunt, and my divorced parents would also be staying there too. Sounds idyllic, right?!

My mum had been suffering with flu whilst in the UK, so she couldn't be with me until she was completely better, so as not to infect me.

After the first chemo session, I didn't feel too bad; I had reacted well to the chemo and other meds, so on the Sunday evening I was allowed to go home, to my aunt's house, where she had made a delicious roast dinner. (She rarely cooks so it was a real treat!)

Over the next few days I was so tired that all I wanted to do was sleep.

A few days later my brother had to return to England. My dad decided he didn't want to leave and was going to stay with me until I was well again.

My mum was due to fly out that week and all my siblings made a pact that every month, one of them would fly out for a couple of weeks, so I always had one of them with me. My grandparents had also arranged to come back to Cyprus and stay until my treatment was over. I felt so blessed and overwhelmed by the love and support around me; It breaks my heart to think that some people have to fight this battle alone.

My mum began researching different holistic methods and the connection of the body's pH levels on cancer, so when she arrived in Cyprus, she made sure we made changes to my diet: no sugar being one of them, so no more chocolates for me!

The first two chemos felt like I bossed it; I thought to myself, okay I've got this. But by the third chemo session was due, I felt worn down and shattered, so I decided I was only going to have one more chemo session and be done with it- I would go down the holistic healing path instead. Absolutely nobody was in agreement with me and as I had already signed a consent form before starting treatment, I reluctantly went for my third chemo. By now, my mum had changed my diet drastically, (I'll go into more detail later), and I had also started taking cannabis oil. The first time I digested the oil, was the first full nights sleep I 'd had in two months. So, alongside the conventional, pharmaceutical treatment, I was also applying a holistic approach.

At the start, I was adamant that having a positive mind set was one of the most important aspects; negative thinking would only make things worse and bring me down, but nothing prepared me for the twists and turns. You start off fighting, raring to go, but gradually it wears you down- It's as though you are holding on to the edge of a cliff and someone is pulling you from your feet. Your grip loosens and you start feeling less in control. The chemo, plus all the other meds start messing with you and you start to feel lost, powerless, empty and vulnerable. The first ten days after chemo everything hurts. When I say everything, I mean everything! I only had to touch my shoulder and it would be agony. Then came more horrible side effects, from excru-ciating headaches to sickness, stomach pains, tooth discolouration and sensitivity, loss of taste and my vision deteriorated. My legs gave way when I got up to walk or stood in the shower; spasms at night, not being able to sleep, losing the sensation in my hands and constipation for days on end. Weight gain (from the steroids), chemo-brain, which is quite literally forgetting words and not being able to talk, because the brain genuinely won't work or function prop-erly. The list is endless and these are just the stand-ard, most common side effects. Not to mention how moody and angry I could get. Mood swings that didn't just swing, they bounced, jumped, rebounded and went something like "Hi!", to "DON'T TALK TO ME!" in a matter of minutes, which I tended to take out on my poor dad. One year later I did apologise to him, but I'll publicly apologise for my Jekyll and Hyde behaviour here too.

One day, I had a craving for a runny boiled egg with some toast to dip into it, so I went off to the kitchen to ask my mum. She looked at me and told me solemnly, that I couldn't have it runny because of salmonella risks, but I could have a hardboiled one instead. Well that was it! I broke down and cried my eyes out because it just wasn't fair! All I wanted was a runny boiled egg and if I couldn't have one then I didn't want anything! Calm down Verucca Salt, I hear the Oompa Loompas saying!

All these feelings and emotions get the better of you, they somehow take control of you and you forget the battle you're in. It's okay to have down days or moments when you feel defeated, but you also have to give yourself a shake and remind yourself this isn't you. It's all the meds, the chemo, the cancer. You can't let it win; remind yourself that **you** are in control, that emotions and feelings come and go.

"Feel the feeling, but don't become the emotion. Witness it. Allow it. Release it." - Crystal Andrus. [24]

In just one moment, you can have that moment of clarity. A friend of mine told me, "The trick is to become aware of when you're thinking a negative thought and instantly switch it to something positive. That just one positive thought outweighs the five negative ones."

You have to remind yourself that you are stronger than this, you are a divine being created by Source with the ability to heal. Dr Bruce Lipton has brought awareness to the subject of the power of thought on the body. Studies have shown that good intentions can have positive physical effects on the body- 'The Placebo effect.' [26]

Dr Joe Dispenza's words always speak volumes to me. A quote from his book, 'Breaking the habit of being yourself: How to lose your mind and create a new one', which I feel is a powerful message:

"Warning: When feelings become the means of thinking, or if we cannot think greater than how we feel, we can never change. To change is to think greater than how we feel. To change is to act greater than the familiar feelings of the memorised self." [25]

So, with that being said, you get back up and you fight again, and again, and again...

After my first chemo, my dad asked me if I wanted to read about the side effects and my answer was no. I believe that if we read something that says the following might happen, we are more likely to manifest it and possibly increase the chances of it actually happening. We might also develop anxiety if we expect the worst to happen. We have all read about the side effects of medication and become a little concerned, especially with the more serious side effects. If we are none the wiser, maybe we will experience less serious side effects.

In fact, there is such a thing as the 'Nocebo effect.' The opposite of the placebo effect, it means the expectation of pain or the negative effects of a medicine. [26] I told my dad that if I was getting any worrying symptoms that concerned me, I would say so, and they could check if it was a listed side effect.

After each chemo, I became weaker, both physically and emotionally. In between the fourth and fifth session I started feeling really drained and it got more difficult to fight. I just wanted to go to sleep and wake up when it was all over. Even eating became a chore. I felt trapped in this new life. I was frustrated that I couldn't do anything for myself; at twenty-eight years old I had to rely on other people to look after me. I felt guilty that my family had put their lives on hold to care for me. I felt my only solace and private time was when I went for a shower. I would turn my music up on my phone, sit on the floor of the shower tray, while the water rained down on my bald head and cry until there were no more tears left. I didn't want to cry in front of my family as I didn't want them to feel any worse or think that I was struggling. As much as I tried to stay positive, there were moments when life became a real struggle. I felt it would have been easier to go to sleep and not wake up again. In these moments of suffering, I would say to myself, please just let me sleep and not wake up, I can't do this anymore. It's times like this when you wake up the next day, in total awe of your body. That even though I, as "Stella", wanted to give up, my body had other plans and kept on fighting, fighting to make me well again. That power within won't let you give up and it's going to keep fighting until the battle has been won.

Even in our darkest moments, comfort can be found in something, or someone; we just have to catch that sparkle of light glistening in the darkness. There is shimmering all around us, if we can just learn to see in the dark. We need to reach out and ask, in those times of darkness. Comfort and love can be found in humour, someone's words, from children, motivational videos, music, a hug, quotes, nature, animals, the night sky. A moment of comfort in difficult times goes a long way.

I know there will be others reading this that can relate and please know you are not alone. The ups, downs and waves of emotions are completely normal. Don't be afraid to reach out and ask for help, and more importantly, remind yourself every day that you will overcome the hurdles and win, no matter who you are or what you are going through!

The chemo sessions took place every three weeks. It's a vicious cycle. You start off feeling okay, ready to fight and with a positive attitude. Then you're pumped with chemo and your whole mood and feelings change in an instant. I would turn up for chemo, positive and ready, but by the end of the day I felt like a completely different person. For the next ten to fourteen days after, you're just not you. It's as though you've been implanted with a different mind, a different mentality; like something else is taking over your mind. Then, after around the two-week mark, you start to feel a bit of normality return and you have a week of "normal", before the next round is due and it starts all over again. By the sixth and final chemo, I thought I was ready for it but this time hit me the hardest. I was well and truly exhausted; I felt sick, tired and had constant stomach pains. I'll never forget lying in bed, sipping endless cups of fresh ginger tea to try to relieve the sickness and my mum squeezing the pressure points in my hand to try to take the edge off the head explosions. All I could do was pray that this would be the last chemo of my life and continued to remind myself that whatever the circumstances, there is always someone else worse off.

Chapter 6

Hair Today, Gone Tomorrow

One of the things I was most afraid of was losing my hair. From the moment that doctor had grabbed my ponytail and told me it would fall out, it haunted me. Even though the doctors were very precise, telling me that my hair would start to fall out three weeks after my first chemo, I refused to believe it and every day I hoped that they had got it wrong. Here I was in denial, refusing to accept. Maybe my body was different, I thought and my hair wouldn't fall out... Wrong!! Exactly three weeks later, I started brushing my hair one morning and clumps of it came out in my hand. I thought to myself, maybe that's all the hair I'll lose. A few days went by and more and more hair was coming out. I was scared to brush it or even touch it. I'll cut it into a bob, I thought to myself, maybe that way

I won't notice it falling out so much. A few hours later I had a trendy long bob. It made no difference; I'd wake up in the morning with hair on my pillow. After showering there would be hair all over the shower tray. I had random balding patches in certain areas; I was traumatised and for the first time I felt angry, sad and powerless. My hair was my mane, my crown. It's bad enough for a man when his hair starts to thin let alone for women. It's what makes us feel feminine. I was so angry. I hated cancer and chemo for taking control of my body. I looked in the mirror staring at the random bald spots on my head. Then the thought crossed my mind to shave it all off myself; I'll take back control. I said out loud to myself, "You're controlling every other part of my body and life, I won't let you take away my hair, I'll do that myself." I wasn't going to wake up every day and look at my hair getting less and less. I was going to be in control of my hair! I walked into the front room and told my parents and aunty my plan. "Umm…okay," my aunty replied, "I'll dig out the clippers."

That evening I sat at the kitchen table, clippers at the ready, my mum, dad and aunty watching nervously. I chopped away with the scissors to get it short enough for the clippers, my mum came over and helped me do the back. I switched on the clippers and started shaving, my aunty stood opposite me, filming the moment, to send to my siblings. My mum, dad and aunty were tearing up, trying not to let me see them getting emotional. I was starting to struggle, so my aunty came and finished it off for me. Fifteen minutes later, it was all gone. They all stared at me. Their faces changed from sadness to joy. "Stel, it actually looks really cool, it suits you." I looked in the mirror and started bawling my eyes out. For the first time, the cancer had got to me, it finally made me cry. My hair really was gone. "Stel, why are you crying? I can't believe how much it actually suits you!" "It doesn't, I hate it!" I cried.

As much as I hated my new shaved look, the feeling of doing it was liberating. Because the hair was so short, I didn't notice it falling out so much... until I looked like a boiled egg.

When you lose your hair, you think that you are going to be living in wigs and that you won't let anyone see you bald; that you will never leave the house without a wig on. I felt as though I looked like an alien and everyone would stare. The reality of it is, chemo gives your head all sorts of feels. One minute it's cold, then it's itchy, then your head's sweating and radiating heat. Having no hair, you can't seem to regulate your body temperature. Even at night, I'd have to wear a ridiculous tea cosy hat just to keep my head warm. I looked like "Where's Wally."

My family back in England put so much effort into sending me wonderful parcels with things to help: a collection of beautiful turbans and headscarves to experiment with, and the most amazing wigs which I thought I would wear 24/7. Time and time again, I tried wearing the wigs, but your head becomes so irritated and sweaty that you think, why am I doing this to myself? With all this going on, it made it unbearable to wear wigs. If you've ever seen the episode of Sex and the City where Samantha, dripping in sweat, rips her wig off her head in the middle of giving a speech and throws it into the audience; that sums it up perfectly!

You get to the point of no longer caring. Chemo makes life complicated enough without having hair and head dramas to worry about. You just want to be comfortable. My most treasured possession was an Adidas baseball cap that my sister gave me. It was easy to wear, comfortable and my go to accessory. I could put it on and take it off easily. That baseball cap will always hold a special place in my heart. Yes, a baseball cap brought me that much joy! Don't get me wrong, there were times when I had to rip that off too, but if you have lost your hair, I can't recommend a baseball cap enough.

As grateful as I am to my family, friends and the people who give support, love and advice, please, please don't tell a cancer patient who has lost their hair, "Don't worry, it will grow back." We know it will grow back, we know we will have hair again one day, but when you've lost all of your hair, that's not what you want to hear. I say this with love, in the hope of helping others to know what to say and what not to say. Hug us, listen to us, cry with us. My nephew, who was only eighteen months old, rubbing my bald head filled me with so much love. My friend sent me a photo of her young daughter playing with Lego. One of the Lego figures' hair had been taken off and she told her mum; "This little girl had cancer like aunty Stella but she's better now." This brought me so much love. Sometimes, children can be our best support team, without even realising it.

By the fourth chemo, my eyebrows and eyelashes started to fall out too. Could this get any worse?! My mum had read about Black Seed oil, (another name for it is Nigella Sativa oil). It is supposed to help with hair loss and hair growth. I started rubbing it on my eyebrows, the very tips of my lashes, (although this was risky, as it would sting if it got in my eyes!), and on my bald head. My eyebrows and lashes stopped falling out and by the last chemo, the hair on my head started to sprout through. I love this magical oil. Even for healthy hair, it's amazing. It has many other health benefits too: It is anti-bacterial, anti-inflammatory, antifungal and has antioxidant properties. It can also help with digestion, builds a stronger immune system, regulates blood sugar levels, balances blood pressure and much more. Black Seed has been used by many cultures for thousands of years, even dating back to Ancient Egyptian times. [2] I take a Black Seed oil capsule daily and have done for the past three years.

So, after the first few months of treatment, I'd lost

my hair and parts of my eyebrows; I was swollen, bloated and had put on so much steroid weight, that none of my clothes fitted me anymore. I was mortified by the way I looked: I looked horrible in my eyes. I wasn't pretty, I wasn't skinny, I wasn't trendy. We now live in a society where appearance and looks have become all that matters, for men too. Social media has programmed us to think that the most important thing is how we look and with the tap of a button, we can edit and filter our appearance to how we want to be perceived. We have become blinded to what's really important. By worrying about what I looked like, I forgot just how amazing my body was: my body was fighting cancer. It took for me to lose all of my "womanly appearance" to realise that it didn't matter what I looked like, or what any of us look like, for that matter.

The egoic mind became still and I came to realise just how much beauty and divinity there is within the human body and how it works continuously to keep us alive. How much beauty there is in kindness, joy and living from our heartspace, through eyes of love. Inside each and every one of us, there is some kind of battle going on and even if we look beautiful, we may not always feel it on the inside. If we could spread kindness and love, if we build each other up instead of judging each other by how we look, we'd live in a much nicer world.

*"If only our eyes saw souls instead of bodies,
how very different our ideals of beauty*

49

would be." Lauren Jauregui [46]

Every morning when I wake up, I smile and express gratitude to my body that I have woken up healthy and well and I thank God for a new day. Try it, you might feel silly at first but I guarantee it will get you smiling, eventually.

Ladies and guys, it's okay to be bald, let the baldness shine through. Be bald and proud! Rock as many looks as you can: hats, turbans, headscarves, tea cosies, wigs, headbands... Have fun with it. I look back now and realise... The bald look, it really wasn't that bad!

Chapter 7

The Diet Switch

Before I was diagnosed, I was clueless on the subject of cancer and the many different aspects of healthy living. I started reading books, listening to podcasts and the teachings of holistic doctors to educate myself. I adopted a healthier lifestyle, which included changing my diet, practising meditation and deep breathing techniques. I also learnt about the importance of gut health, and how the gut must be cleansed in order to begin the healing process. Dr Sebi teaches that certain acidic foods can create mucus and inflammation in the body, which can lead to sickness and ill health. [35] Dr Sebi is one of my favourite holistic doctors and teaches about the benefits of healing by creating an alkaline state. I gained more knowledge about various topics, on my cancer journey, than I ever did at school. I truly believe that these things should be taught at school, instead of some of the pointless topics we learn about. Why are we not being taught about the discoveries of pioneers like Nikola Tesla and Dr Otto Warburg; or how to eat healthy, by growing our own food? I'm sure this knowledge would be more beneficial to us, rather than learning about the history of the Tudors and Stuarts or how to play a recorder.

The human body is made up of millions of cells. For most of us, our body's natural defence system (the immune system), knows how to fight foreign bodies and keep us healthy. [3] Dr David Servan-Schreiber explains that there are several factors we can adhere to for a healthier and stronger immune system, such as managing our stress responses, healthier life-styles such as exercise, better diet, and less toxins. [4] As Louise Hay also mentions in her book 'You Can Heal Your Life', emotions can also play a role in our health and wellbeing. One of the most import-ant factors for me, and something I believe every-one should take into consideration, is what Dr Otto Warburg says: cancer cannot survive in an alkaline environment. So don't forget, negative thoughts, emotions and constant stress can also have a detri-mental effect on the body, but in this chapter I'm going to talk about diet.

The first step I took, was the process of starving the cancer of sugars, unhealthy carbohydrates, dairy and meat which can all affect the pH level of the body. This is why many holistic practitioners rec-ommend switching to a vegan diet when it comes to getting the body back to good health. We are led to believe that we need meat as part of our diet and maybe back in caveman days, when we had limited DNA strands, that was so, but we have evolved an awful lot since then. Dr Dean Ornish and Nobel prize winner Elizabeth Blackburn found that a vegan diet and lifestyle changes, such as regular exercise and stress management, caused more than five hundred genes to change in a few months, switching on genes that prevent illness and disease, and turning off genes that cause illness and disease. [5] As Dr David Servan-Schreiber says in his book, cancer feeds on sugar. This includes foods such as pasta, bread, white rice, and any foods that contain white flour. These are foods with a high glycemic index so once consumed, the blood levels of glucose rise rapidly. [4]

Dairy... Let's be honest, do we really need to drink the breast milk of another animal?! Human beings are the only species to continue the consumption of milk after weaning from a baby and to drink the milk of another animal. Cows milk contains hormones and proteins that is administered for an eighty pound calf, not a human baby. [42]

Although there is information out there that states that there is no link between dairy and mucus; (which I believe is due to the fact that the dairy industry is a multimillion pound business and to lose customers would cost them dearly;) some studies have shown that dairy products can produce excess mucus in the body. Most dairy products contain protein molecules called casein which can increase mucus secretions. [6] Lactose, is the main sugar found in milk. In humans, the enzyme LACTASE, which breaks down lactose, stops being produced when the person is aged between two and five. Undigested sugars end up in the colon, where they begin to ferment and produce gas. [43] Is it any wonder so many people are lactose intolerant?! In my experience, when my diet included dairy, I would suffer from terrible acne and sinus problems, but since cutting back on dairy, my skin and airways are clear.

A healthy pH level is around the 7 mark; if the pH is below 6 it is considered to be moving into the acidic zone, which is when we can develop health problems. You can also become too alkaline which is called alkalosis, so it is important to find a healthy all-round balance that suits you. As mentioned in the book, 'The Acid Alkaline Food Guide', there are several different factors that affect the pH level of the body and several ways of maintaining an acid-alkaline balance.

Meat is considered a very high acid-forming food, which is why I recommend the vegan diet. [7] Purines are natural compounds found in the body, but are also present in some foods such as animal proteins, seafoods, certain types of dried beans, sugars and alcohol. High amounts of purine can form uric acid, which is then filtered through the kidneys and execreted through the urine. If there is too much uric acid present, the kidneys are not fully able to function as well to get rid of it and uric acid can build up in the blood causing acidity. [44]

Cancer can also be affected by oxygen levels. A healthy body loves oxygen but cancer cells do not. Cancer cells love glucose. The German doctor Otto Warburg discovered that all forms of cancer are characterised by two basic conditions: acidosis (having an acidic pH level) and lack of oxygen (hypoxia). "Where you have one, you have the other." Warburg said, "If you deprive a cell 35% of its oxygen for forty-eight hours, it may become cancerous." He also discovered that cancer cells can live without oxygen. A lower pH which is acidic means less oxygen getting to the cells of the body, conditions where cancer cells can thrive. Warburg discovered that as cancer cells do not breathe oxygen, they cannot survive in an environment of high oxygen levels, otherwise known as an alkaline state, therefore it is important to get high levels of oxygen into the body. Dr Warburg won a Nobel prize for this discovery in 1931. [8] What an epic discovery by an amazing man. If Warburg discovered this root cause of cancer back in 1931, why are we still trying to find cures for cancer? Personally, I think he made it perfectly clear what is needed to keep a body healthy and free of the disease.

Things like exercising and deep breathing can help with getting oxygen into the body. I use a type of deep breathing called oxycise, which I find to be very effective. Joe Dispenza's breathing technique, taken from his book, 'Becoming Supernatural', is also beneficial for me. The Wim Hof breathing technique is one of my favourites; it can take a bit of practise but has tremendous health benefits. [9] If you don't know Wim Hof, get to know him, he is awesome! I definitely want to be just like him when I grow up!

Shockingly, statistics taken in September 2018 by Cancer Research UK, have shown that the estimated lifetime cancer risk is one in two people. [17] But! We can each do our part to try and change, or even prevent this, through diet, lifestyle changes, becoming more mindful, more aware of our emotions and how we deal with life.

"Every 35 days, your skin replaces itself and your body makes new cells from the foods you eat. What you eat, literally becomes you." Unknown [27]

Changing your diet can be one of the hardest things, believe me I know, especially when you love chocolate and all things sweet! It's all about breaking habits. After a few weeks of cutting out sugar, I realised that I didn't even crave it anymore. Once you start to eat better, over time you'll notice an improvement in digestion, mood (except if you're on chemo meds!), mental focus, increased energy and a general improvement in health. [10]

Acidic forming foods include refined foods, for example: bread, cakes, pastries, foods with a long shelf life, ready meals, fizzy drinks, alcohol, coffee, meats, fish, sugar, dairy, fried foods and all processed foods. [7] I know, I can hear you all moaning- I did too.

I'm going to mention some superfoods, but if you do your own research you will find many more. It is said, that our diet should contain around 80% of alkaline forming foods, and 20% of acidic forming foods if our pH level is moderately or highly acidic. If our pH level is in the healthy range, 35% to 40% of our food intake should be acidic forming, once digested, and 60% to 65% alkaline forming. Almost all vegetables are alkalising and the majority of fruits too. [7] In the book 'The Acid Alkaline Food Guide', although tomatoes are not listed as an alkaline forming food, they are listed as low acidity forming and their health benefits are excellent. Tomatoes are full of nutrients, improve heart health and contain lycopene that has been shown to help protect against cancer. Cooked tomatoes provide more lycopene than raw tomatoes. [11]

Carrots, avocados, peppers, sweet potatoes and leafy greens such as kale, spinach, romaine lettuce and parsley are all alkaline forming. [7] They are versatile ingredients and you can do lots with them. Beetroots are amazing, you can have them in salads, soups or smoothies. They improve blood health, support liver health, have anti-cancer benefits and much more. Just remember when you've eaten them as you may get a shock when you see the colour of your pee! [11] Make your dishes more exciting by using turmeric, cumin, ginger, garlic, onions and bay leaves. Pomegranates are delicious and the seeds benefit heart and blood health. Pineapples contain an enzyme called bromelain which has been shown to have anti-inflammatory effects. [11]

A few other alkaline foods include: apples, blueberries, blackberries, lentils, okra, papaya, kiwi, hemp seeds, almonds and cashews. [7]

If you're stuck with what to substitute pasta, rice and unhealthy carbohydrates for, try grains such as wild rice, jasmine rice, bulgur wheat and quinoa. Potatoes are also an alkaline forming food, unless you fry them into chips or fries! [7]

Chickpeas are one of my favourite foods and you can do so much with them: curries, stews, burgers and they can even be used to make desserts. Chickpeas are rich in vitamins, minerals, fibre and protein and offer many other health benefits. [12]

Spirulina and chlorella are freshwater algae with exceptional health benefits- they are packed with proteins, vitamins and nutrients. Spirulina has been shown to improve immune health, containing powerful antioxidant and anti-inflammatory properties. It contains the compound phycocyanin which can protect cells from damage. Chlorella is rich in chlorophyll which helps cleanse the blood of toxins. [13] You can buy them as a powder or in tablet/capsule form. I take two spirulina chlorella capsules daily.

I know this all seems so unexciting, switching from what we know as "yummy" foods to "boring, healthy" foods and it can seem like a drag, but if I can do it, you can too! There are so many options out there nowadays, with vegan lifestyle on the rise it gives you a chance to experiment and try new things. Don't just take my word for it, do your own research and learn for yourselves. I discovered that if we try to make drastic changes, it may be too much to do all at once. It's easier to make small changes to our diet and lifestyle gradually, over time.

I love finding new recipes and trying things I wouldn't normally think of trying: mushroom and lentil bolognese, chickpea burgers, sweet potato chocolate brownies. Trust me, they're much more delicious than you would imagine! Besides, new challenges can be fun and exciting. Take yourself out of your comfort zone. 'Bosh' have amazing recipe books and the meals are so exciting and tasty! Their Instagram page is 'bosh.tv' and they are always posting new exciting recipes to try. I will post a link to their website. [28]

A typical day for me starts with drinking about a litre of water, before having my morning coffee, followed by my own homemade chia pudding. (The recipes can be found on my Instagram page, 'theb0 dytalks'). I try to incorporate raw and cooked foods into my daily diet, so for lunch I'll have a smoothie followed by nuts, dates, fruit, raw veg and pitta bread with hummus or guacamole; I snack on this throughout the day. Dinner usually consists of carbs such as: quinoa, potatoes, rice noodles, bulgur wheat or wild rice, mixed with legumes or beans such as: chickpeas, lentils, adzuki beans, black eyed peas, butter beans etc. Sometimes I will add a bit of tofu and on the odd occasion some halloumi cheese and to finish it off, I'll add vegetables or greek salad. A few of my favourite dinners are: chickpeas, cooked in a spicy tomato sauce, with spinach, cauliflour, green beans and babycorn, teamed with quinoa; mixed beans, veg and potatoe stew; butter beans, slow cooked in the oven with sweet potatoes, celery, carrots, courgettes and broccoli; lentil and mushroom stroganoff with mashed potatoes; and falafel wrap with tahini and greek salad. Don't get me wrong, if I fancy something, I'll eat it and I definitely have my junk food and takeaway days. I don't think we should deprive ourselves of things altogether, because that's how bad diets and insecurities with food can start. If I want to eat a piece of chocolate, some cake or crisps now and then, I will, but I'm much more aware of how much of it I eat nowadays. I don't like the idea of labelling ourselves vegan, veggie, pescetarian or carnivores, I feel this creates division, when there's really no need. I know people who eat vegan all week and then eat meat on the weekends; similarly, there are meat eaters who try to not eat meat a few times a week. Each to their own. There is no set rule for each individual diet, just find what's right for you and become more mindful of what you eat. However, if the body is in an acidic state and sickness is present, an alkaline diet is recommended, to bring the body back to a neutral state.

To end this chapter, I'm going to talk about my favourite discovery... coconuts! Coconut water, coconut milk, coconut oil, coconut sugar. All things coconut! But most importantly, coconut water, fresh out of young coconuts, which are green or orange in colour; coconut water was a Godsend. My mum had discovered, during her research, that drinking the water from fresh, young coconuts can relieve the side effects of chemo and electrolytes found in the water help to replenish cells.

Once the top of the coconut is cut off, the water should be consumed straight away. Fresh young coconut water contains amino acids, minerals such as potassium, chloride, calcium, magnesium, phosphorus, sodium and is a great source of antioxidant protection. [14]

I started drinking coconut water during my third chemo; I would drink the water from one coconut two days before chemo, one on the morning of chemo, another when I got home from chemo and then one a day for the next five days. It helped with the nausea, stomach upsets and headaches. A family friend that travelled abroad for work, very kindly brought us the fresh coconuts, as they weren't available in Cyprus. It worked wonders for me and helped me feel better much quicker.

Coconut oil, virgin or raw organic is what I would use daily and still do. I put it in my coffee, smoothies, cook with it and use it as a moisturiser. I also used coconut oil alongside the cannabis oil that I was taking as part of my holistic approach.

Cannabis is said to be one of the most healing plants. The human body is made up of an endocannabinoid system with receptors designed to process the cannabinoids in the cannabis plant. Studies have shown that cannabis has anti-cancer effects as well as many other health benefits. [15] In fact, we are introduced to cannabinoids as newborns. A number of scientific studies have found that human breast milk contains some of the same cannabinoids found in the cannabis plant, which is vital for human development. [40]

I was pointed in the direction of Rick Simpson, who has a specific method for taking cannabis oil medicinally, which gave me a better understanding of the oil consumption. [19] The documentary on YouTube, 'Healing cancer with cannabis: The Rick Simpson story', [20] was also something I found very interesting. I made sure I read as much as possible about medicinal cannabis oil and did lots of research prior to using cannabis oil. It was so important for me to educate myself fully on this topic, first and foremost.

One of the hardest things for me to give up throughout treatment was sugar! Anyone that knows me, knows how much I love chocolate and how much I could eat, so whenever I needed a sugar fix, my mum would bake me healthy little sweet treats, using dates, bananas or carob syrup. Once treatment was over, I started using coconut sugar for my coffee and baking. Coconut sugar is a better alternative than regular white sugar, but of course it is still a sugar, so should be used sparingly. Coconut sugar is normally a light brown colour and has more of a caramel taste. Also, it does not taste as sweet as regular cane sugar. Coconut sugar is made from the sap of the coconut and retains some of its nutrients. The most notable nutrients found in coconut sugar include, zinc, calcium and potassium, however, you would need to eat a ton of the stuff to get these nutrients in meaningful amounts. [16] Don't do it sugar lovers!

Chapter 8

Laughter is the Best Medicine

Thanks to the teachings of several experts, such as: Dr Bruce Lipton, Dr Bradley Nelson, Louise Hay and Dr Joe Dispenza, I discovered that emotions can have a massive effect on how we are feeling and how we react in certain situations... Knowledge is power!

This experience has also guided me towards a more spiritual path, leading me to a higher awakening and a deeper understanding of how negative emotions can affect our chakras and the energy that flows through our bodies. I always had an open mind regarding spirituality and energy work, but I had also been sceptical too.

A few months prior to my diagnosis, during the summer, I went for a chakra cleanse with my friends, at a spiritual event. I was so sceptical and thought, how could she possibly "cleanse" my chakras using crystals and energy?! A bit hypocritical seeing as I had collected crystals as a child. Anyway, I sat in a chair and after several minutes the practitioner said to me: "Your left side is completely blocked and I can't seem to clear it. I'm all about natural healing, but I really think you should see a doctor." Unfortunately, I didn't give it much thought and got on with my life as normal. It wasn't until halfway through my treatment, that this came to me randomly in passing thought one day; I then remembered everything the lady had said. It was the trigger to an awakening within me and in that moment, everything changed. I felt inspired to learn more about chakras, crystals and energy work; to act from love and release any negative emotions; to be more intuitive, to meditate and learn about breathing techniques. Coincidentally, around the same time, a family friend gave me a healing quartz crystal, which was nicely played by the Universe! Crystals are now a part of my daily life and have all sorts of different uses: healing, protection, self-care, grounding and energy clearing. Nowadays I go willingly for chakra cleansing sessions and with a totally open mind. It's also become an important part of my lifestyle to chakra cleanse myself and friends too. These amazing natural stones, that are part of our beautiful Earth's make-up, have powerful energy and are used in so many ways. In fact, quartz crystals are widely used in electronics, and quartz resonators are used as high performance resonators for use in filters and oscillators. [47] I feel a strong sense of gratitude to this lady, who I initially doubted, and although I didnt realise at the time, she definitely planted a seed that needed to grow.

As previously mentioned, I had a build-up of resentment eating away at me; as much as I had tried to forgive my ex-partner, I just couldnt let go of the resentment. After my awakening, I was finally able to let go, to truly forgive. Something inside of me changed and all I felt was love for all beings. I felt a closeness to God that I had never felt before and a loving peace within. I realised that holding on to negative, lower vibrational emotions, was only damaging me and my wellbeing.

Once I was able to truly listen to my body, to tune in to my heart chakra and find alignment, I felt God's love, and only then was I able to finally let go of the past. I was seeing things through the eyes of love and compassion and realised that we are all just trying to deal with our own inner turmoils. Instead of feeling negative emotions towards others, we should try to be compassionate and forgiving. Someones unacceptable behaviour may be due to their own inner conflicts and issues that they are unsure how to deal with. If someone upsets or angers us, maybe it is a chance for us to try to learn something about ourselves, to learn how to react differently; they are only acting as a mirror to show us what needs to be healed within ourselves. Everyone we meet is for a reason, so look for what each person is trying to show you, because there are always lessons to be learnt. It sure took me a long time to realise this! Maybe, if we were more aware of our emotions, we would realise that holding onto negativity does more harm than good. If children were taught these things from an early age, if we could learn about our feelings and emotions, how to deal with life lessons and situations in a mindful way, maybe then, it might be easier for us to treat others with love, kindness and compassion.

It wasn't until recently that I read a book by Louise Hay, 'You Can Heal Your Life'. An amazing book, by an amazing author! She talks about diseases as dis-ease, in other words, unease within the body. She lists the problem/illness/dis-ease, the probable cause and the new thought pattern to tell yourself. An excerpt from her book: "**Cancer-** *Deep Hurt. Long-standing resentment. Deep secret or grief eating away at the self. Carrying hatreds. What's the use? - I lovingly forgive and release all of the past. I choose to fill my world with joy. I love and approve of myself.*" [31] As I read this, my jaw dropped, I couldn't believe how

69

much this rang true for me.

Abraham Hicks came up with something called: The Emotional Guidance Scale. Her book, 'Ask and It Is Given' gives you a good understanding of lower and higher vibrational emotions. She lists the emotions from joy, appreciation, empowerment, freedom and love at the top of the scale at number one, and down at the bottom of the scale at number twenty-two is fear, grief, depression, despair and powerlessness. [32] For me, this scale has been a great reference in my life. You can learn to work up the scale to achieve more positive, joyful emotions. Obviously, you can't jump from fear to joy, but you can take baby steps to get yourself there. When you learn to live from these elevated emotions, you can feel the happiness and love resonate within you. You can be brought to tears of pure love and gratitude from experiencing life this way. It's a feeling I cannot explain, only you yourself can feel this bliss. As I said previously, the benefits of healing are magical, once we get through the darkness and reach the light on the other side.

"For most people, their spiritual teacher is their suffering. Because eventually, the suffering brings about awakening." Eckhart Tolle [36]

Dr Joe Dispenza is someone else whose studies and books have had a huge impact on my life. In his book 'Becoming Supernatural' he talks about a lady that tragically lost her husband to suicide. Every time she thought about it, the body couldnt tell the difference between the memory of it and the actual incident, so she was producing the same chemistry in her brain and body, as if she was reliving this stressful event over and over again. When we are faced with a dangerous situation and need to react with fight or flight, the body releases cortisol and adrenalin to help us in this stressful situation. However, Joe Dispenza says that many of us spend most of our time in heightened stress mode due to work, financial or family issues, so the stress hormones keep pumping through our body, and we stay on high alert instead of returning to balance. Constant stress down-regulates the healthy expression of genes, which can lead to disease. "In fact our bodies become so conditioned to this rush of chemicals that they become addicted to them" - Joe Dispenza. Dispenza also says that elevated feelings could signal new genes to make healthy proteins. [21] Practising meditation and being present and aware can help us achieve a healthier mind, body and soul. Joe Dispenza also offers a variety of different meditation exercises in this book, which I have found to be beneficial.

Meditation and understanding the chakras (also known as the energy centres of our body), isn't something that everyone gets right away. It took me a long time to understand the benefits and the way it works and an even longer time to still the chatter in my mind. Even now I have moments in which I can't quiet the mind, but it's all a part of learning awareness and becoming more mindful. It is completely normal to become distracted in meditation but this doesn't mean we have failed. In the moment of noticing distraction, you can no longer be distracted. Recognise it and once again gently guide yourself back to the point of focus. Each time we focus, we are building our awareness and concentration. The more we practice building our focus, we are increasing our capacity to enhance connection to the present moment. There's so much help out there: YouTube, books, podcasts, yoga and meditation classes, even Instagram if you follow the right accounts. Anyone can get the hang of it and feel the benefits, it just takes some practice, solitude and lots of self-love.

Surprisingly, one of the most important things throughout my cancer journey was laughter and it became part of our daily life. "Laughter is the best medicine after all." Research has shown that your thoughts and being optimistic can have an influence on your immunity. [18]

> "The Primary cause of unhappiness is never the situation, but your thoughts about it. Be aware of the thoughts you are thinking." - Eckhart Tolle, A new Earth: Awakening to your life's purpose [34]

Something that kept popping into my head, was what my friend had said to me previously: "Stel, just remember, all it takes is one positive thought to override all negative thoughts." I know at times it may seem hard, but it's all about teaching the mind to see the positive instead of the negative, to become more aware of our thoughts. The same way we train other body parts and muscles, we can also train the brain. Shawn Achor, author of 'The Happiness Advantage', says that you can rewire the brain to become happy, simply by writing down three things you're grateful for everyday for twenty-one days. [29]

I was very lucky to have my family and friends around,doing silly things to make me laugh and keep my spirits lifted. They would walk into the room wearing my wigs, (brothers, dad, aunt, cousins, nephew!), singing, dancing, doing silly routines and putting on shows for me. We laughed so much, in spite of it all! One of my friends would video himself doing karaoke and send me the videos, which had me in absolute stitches. Once the chemo had finished and I started feeling a bit stronger, my friends Titos and Faidra would take me out once a week, for a day trip to boost my spirits. My best friend since childhood flew out from the UK to surprise me. The shock of seeing her probably did wonders for my immune system! We had endless laughs, with my cousin joining us too. The three of us dressing up in my turbans and headscarves, reminiscing, laughing, joking and taking endless selfies. My family and friends in the UK also sent me cards and little gifts to cheer me up. Another of my best friends in England ran a marathon in my name, to raise money for a cancer charity. Everyone did so much to boost my morale and support me which it certainly did. I am eternally grateful for every ounce of love I received. I watched comedies and endless episodes of Friends and Impractical Jokers, anything that would make me giggle and get me laughing. Whatever you can do to make yourself smile to release the endorphins, do it! Laughter really was a big part of my recovery.

As children we laugh so much more and let joy into our lives more freely. As adults, we seem to forget the importance of laughter, and life becomes much more serious. No matter our age or circumstances, we should always remember how important and joyous laughter is; to try to laugh as much as we can, on a daily basis. The inner child within us, that wants to have fun, never goes away, unless we neglect it and lose touch. Allow the inner child to stay ageless.

Of course, it's okay to have down days or low moments, but the most important thing is to remember not to stay there. Pick yourself back up again, remind yourself that every situation is temporary. Trust me, you're stronger than you think you are. The body already knows it, it's only the mind we have to convince.

> *"Your mind will always believe everything*
> *you tell it. Feed it faith. Feed it truth. Feed*

it with love." Unknown. [30]

Chapter 9

Life Changes

The final hurdle was radiotherapy. I finished chemotherapy and had a month break to rebuild my strength back up, before starting a month of radiotherapy. Although radiotherapy was going to be one month of daily treatments, I thought it would be a breeze compared to the effects of chemo. The worst part of the radiotherapy treatment was having to wear a mask which is moulded to fit the shape of your head and neck in order to hold you in the correct position. It looked like a plastic mesh with tiny holes all over and one slightly bigger hole for your mouth. I looked and felt like something out of a Hannibal Lecter movie. It was horribly claustrophobic, but apart from feeling tired I was blessed not to experience any side effects.

Once radiotherapy finished, I had to wait twelve weeks before I could go for a PET scan to see if treatment had been successful. Those twelve weeks were probably the worst; it became a waiting game and all sorts of thoughts were going through my mind. As much as you try to remain positive and have faith, there's always going to be times when worrying thoughts and fear pop up. This is when living mindfully and positively really comes into practice and tests you to the limit. Meditation is key!

After chemo had finished, I had a CT scan to check the size of the tumour. As I sat with my specialist, he said to me, "Stella, the tumour has shrunk from the size of two fists to just four centimetres. That's an incredible result, we didnt expect the chemotherapy to shrink it this much! Maybe your body had an excellent reaction to the therapy." I wanted to tell him all about the power of the mind, meditation, emotions, diet and cannabis oil, but I just sat there smiling knowingly. I had mentioned holistic approaches previously, but they had made it clear that it was not something they were willing to discuss, so I just kept it to myself. I knew that it wasn't just the chemo that had shrunk the tumour!

Before radiotherapy began, my radio oncologist looked at the before and after scan, to see what she was going to be dealing with. As my mum and I sat in her office, she looked at the computer screen, then at me, then back at the screen again, a puzzled look on her face. She then left the room, before returning a few minutes later. She sat back down and said, "This is a dramatic reduction in the size of the tumour, we wouldn't have expected this from chemotherapy alone." My mum and I just looked at each other and smiled, we both knew what the other was thinking; we were convinced that the alternative approach had also played a role in my recovery. Never doubt your inner power, it's the magic of your soul. You have to really believe in yourself and want to make the changes necessary, in order to heal.

Twelve long weeks later, I flew to the UK to have a PET scan as there wasn't a machine available in Cyprus. The results were forwarded to my specialist in Cyprus, who said he'd contact me once he'd reviewed them.

Going to England for the scan was a blessing in disguise, as it gave me something to look forward to during those twelve weeks of waiting. Some of my family didn't know I was coming back, so I got to surprise them. I'll never forget my aunty, uncle and grandma's reactions when they saw me; I'll treasure those memories forever.

On the twenty second of November 2016, I received a phone call from my aunty back in Cyprus. "I just got off the phone to your doctor," she said, "The cancer has gone. You're free!" I broke down crying, tears streaming down my face. I felt every emotion, from disbelief to relief, shock, happiness and joy. It was an utterly surreal moment. What a rollercoaster ride it had been!

Christmas 2016 was so special. To spend the holidays with all my loved ones was truly a blessing.

Life is a magical gift and we should cherish every day, instead of taking it for granted. We shouldn't have to experience something bad in order for us to appreciate the true value of life.

One evening, my cousins arranged a get together with my siblings and one of our closest friends. I felt so lucky and blessed to be sat there with them, enjoying each other's company that I was completely taken by surprise when they brought out a massive chocolate cake, bigger than my head, with the words, "Well done Stella, you kicked cancer's butt!" written on it. The look on my face said it all. The love I felt inside was bursting out of me. And I got to dig into a huge chocolate cake!

Cancer completely changes your life, as well as you as a person. Nothing can prepare you for what's coming and of course, everyone's journey is different.

My life changed dramatically overnight, from living a "normal" life, to then have to leave my job, my home, my friends, my hobbies and all the things I enjoyed doing. To be isolated from the outside world and the life I was living, to watch everyone else carrying on with their lives as normal, was so difficult. Everything is turned upside down and then, suddenly you find that you can't even take care of yourself, but to be alienated from the life you were living makes it ten times harder. As lucky and grateful as I am to have had the amazing support of family and friends, you can't help but feel alone. No one can truly understand what you are going through or feeling inside. There's no real support for the different emotions you're going through and different phases you experience. You're diagnosed, treatment begins and off you go. Although the nurses and doctors were amazing and always there if I felt unwell, it would have been comforting to have some kind of support group with others around my age. To have the opportunity to discuss the impact and upheaval it has on your life as a young adult and the changes you have to make.

Obviously it is extremely difficult for those closest to you too: your family, friends and loved ones; it's a situation that has an impact on everyone in your life.

My parents gave up their everyday lives and jobs in England to be by my side, to support and take care of me. My siblings flew out to be with me whenever they could take time off work and held the fort down back home, whilst also looking out for each other. My aunty in Cyprus shared her home and love with us all and spent countless hours in the hospital with me. The rest of my family, back in England, had to deal with it all from thousands of miles away, receiving updates from the others on a daily basis. My grandparents were incredibly supportive also. Although they had been through a similar experience with my mother, who was diagnosed with cancer at fifteen years old, they still managed to put on a brave face, despite their past experience and the painful memories it invoked. Everyone around you needs support too. All they can do is watch, as the person they love is suffering and there's nothing they can do to make it stop. To watch someone you love go through pain and not be able to help, is painful in itself. As much as they try to put on a brave face and remain positive, you can still see the pain in their eyes. At least for yourself, you know what you are going through and the ways in which you have to deal with it, whereas all they can do is watch. Cancer doesn't just affect you, it affects everyone around you too.

Something else I really struggled with, was the thought of children having to go through this hell. A couple of times I saw young children going through chemo and it broke my heart.

Around ten months after receiving the all clear, I decided I wanted to do a skydive for charity and my cousin Luna said she wanted to support me by doing it together. We had an absolute blast! It's an experience I'll cherish forever. To top it off, we raised 3,500 Euros for the charity, "One dream, one wish", a charity in Cyprus that supports children going through cancer and other illnesses. They focus on the wish or dream of the child, and offer financial and psychological support for the children and their families. This was the perfect charity for me to raise money for.

Afterwards, my cousin and I were invited to the charity to meet some of the children and to hear their stories. I cannot even begin to describe how much it affected us, it was soul destroying. From that day on, I vowed to help spread awareness of everything I had learnt and to one day, hopefully start my own charitable support days for children and young adults. A retreat, for them to temporarily escape what they are going through and to learn the importance of holistic healing and the power of the mind.

November, 2020 was the fourth year that I had been in remission. Personally, I don't really like to think of it as being "in remission"; I feel as though this means cancer still has an ongoing hold on my life and that it's not really over yet. I see it as something in my life that I had to overcome in order to learn, to grow and generally change my life for the better. Every experience we go through is to teach us something, if we are willing to learn. Bad things don't happen to you, they happen for you. Your pain is your teacher. This was a gift in order to begin my path to awakening and to help others.

Cancer is a part of my past, it is not going to be a part of my future and nor should it be a part of yours either. I wake up every day and tell myself I am healthy and thank my body for keeping me that way. But most importantly, you really have to believe that you are healthy and well. The power of the mind can enslave you or empower you! I am consciously aware of how I take care of my mind, body and soul. You cannot take care of only your body and expect results if you are not taking care of your mind and soul. What good is a healthy body without a healthy mind and soul? When these three are in harmony, they are a powerful force, so it's important to nurture and give attention to each of them in order for us to be in alignment and live as we were created to... A self regulating organism with the ability to heal.

These last four years, since getting the all clear, have been the best years of my life, I've learnt so much and continue to do so. I've changed and grown, mentally and spiritually, constantly evolving. There's always room for learning, changing and personal growth. Life's lessons are infinite and part of our souls evolution.

I've travelled and met some amazing people from different parts of the world which has been the start of beautiful, new friendships. People that I feel a soul connection with, a strong recognition and knowing they will be a part of my future. For me, this just goes to show, no matter what our background or where we're from, when we feel a connection with someone our soul recognises this.

I have awoken spiritually and discovered that true peace and happiness is found within. Expecting to find happiness and contentment through others, or in the material world, only brings temporary satisfaction.

Inner healing, also known as "shadow work", is an important part of our spiritual growth and the healing journey. Setting aside time to be alone, to focus on our inner self, can help us to confront and deal with our insecurities, past mistakes, repressed emotions; to unlearn ingrained learnt behaviours and repetitive patterns. It's learning to accept the pain and feelings that arise instead of burying them away. Of course, this can sometimes be a painful and emotional process, as everything in need of healing, must be brought into our conscious awareness and that can be difficult; but it can bring about an enlightening rebirth. Once we become fully aware of our shadow self, we can learn to deal with it in a mindful way, to treat ourselves the same way we would a child, with love, compassion and forgiveness. Tell yourself that it's normal to feel uncomfortable emotions, that making mistakes is part of life's learning process and to start each new day afresh. Every day is a new opportunity to become a better you and leave the past behind; to love, forgive and nurture yourself the same way you would a child. Imagine yourself talking to your inner child, with compassion and understanding, telling them that you love and forgive them, that it's safe to feel uncomfortable emotions. Also, forgiving others that may have impacted our lives in a negative way can help us to heal. When we forgive, we can let go of the hold it has over us. Holding onto pain, anger, negative emotions and suffering, is like holding out an object in your hand; over time, it will feel heavier and heavier, until your hand begins to ache, as it cannot withstand the weight any longer. Imagine placing the painful emotion or memory onto a cloud, slowly watching it drift away into the Universe and allowing a cloud of love and positivity to take its place. You might feel a bit silly at first and it can be difficult to believe new thought patterns can be achieved, so repeating affirmations to yourself is a great way to train your mind to believe what you are saying. The brain is like a computer, it can be programmed to behave how we want it to. For example, if we write, repeat or listen to positive affirmations daily, such as: "I am free of worry and regret... I forgive myself and others... I am proud of myself... I am in charge of how I feel", eventually it will be programmed into our brain until we start to believe it. This is all part of healing and loving ourselves, nurturing the soul. Once we learn to fully love ourselves in a soulful way, we can find the happiness that emanates from within and share it with the world. We will be able to fill up our own cup rather than expecting someone, or something to fill it. Don't get me wrong, there are still days when I am tested and have to consciously remind myself to breathe deeply, to remember that there's always a lesson to be learnt, and that this is all a part of life's journey. Who would we be without life's trials and tribulations? It sure makes for a more exciting ride. One of my favourite quotes that left a lasting impression on me...

*"We are here to change the world. Not just follow
rules, earn money and die." Unknown.* [33]

I know that evolving into the ever changing world
of technology, pharmaceuticals, mass food produc-
tion, transport, the pace and speed of life etc.
is a natural path for human progression, but we
shouldn't lose touch with ancient knowledge. Curi-
ously, many ancient civilisations were far more in
tune, spiritually and holistically, than we are now.
They understood that spending time outdoors and
connecting with nature is vital for the body, mind
and soul. It also strengthened their spiritual senses
and they always gave something back to the Earth,
to show their gratitude and respect. Living this way
also helped them to live in the moment and be more
present, instead of dwelling on the past or worrying
about the future. The ancients also walked barefoot and believed Earth's energy could be absorbed
through the soles of our feet. "Grounding" or "earth-
ing", is when we walk barefoot on soil, grass, rocks,
sand; natural surfaces. It has been shown to enhance health and well-being, due to the transfer of
free electrons from the Earth's surface that spreads
throughout our tissues. Its effects have been shown
to be a powerful antioxidant. Wearing shoes all the
time disconnects us from the Earth's energy flow;
if you think about it, this is why it always feels so
good when we walk barefoot on the beach or grass
or go paddling in the sea! [39]

Their medicines, treatments and remedies also came from nature, from herbs and plants.

"For every human illness, somewhere in the world there exists a plant which is the cure." Rudolph Steiner [37]

Oregano oil, colloidal silver, garlic, olive leaf extract and echinacea are just some of natures best antibiotics and each one treats a different ailment. Oregano oil has been shown to fight bacterial, fungal and yeast infections. Colloidal silver is good for ear infections, skin problems such as psoriasis and pneumonia. Echinacea is known for its anti-bacterial properties and is excellent for upper respiratory tract infections and colds. Natural antibiotics are also more appealing to me as they don't disrupt the gut flora, unlike pharmaceutical antibiotics. [38]

The ancient knowledge we need is out there, waiting for us to rediscover it and reconnect again. Escape the modern world and take some tips from the Ancients. Perhaps we could live more of a disease-free life, full of abundance and goodness. It really is possible and the power lies within you.

So, as I come to the end of my book, my only hope is that it has helped you, even in the smallest way. If you know somebody that's going through a tough time, be it cancer, illness, depression, or whatever else, I hope they may find some comfort and knowledge reading this book. I hope I have been able to give people an insight into what a cancer patient goes through emotionally and physically, so that they, and their loved ones, might have a better insight and understanding. I hope and pray that we can all become more aware of emotions, diet, lifestyle and inner healing.

In a world where all we hear about is negativity, hatred and division being constantly spread by the media, let's focus on coming together, to spread love, kindness and joy. Let's educate ourselves to learn to better ourselves and our children. Let's be passionate about life and concentrate on all the good that goes on in the world, rather than all the doom and gloom. Let's all help each other and do our part, in any way possible, to become more enlightened and united, in order to create a better world. A new Earth. A better world and future for our children, and our children's children. What a beautiful place that would be. A world full of love. After all, love is the highest frequency. Love wins!

References

[1] Elster, N. 2014. Chemotherapy: from world war to the war on cancer. [Online]. [07 February 2020]. Available from:https://www.theguardian.com/science/blog/2014/oct/08/chemotherapy-world-war-cancer-mustard-gas#top

[2] Group, E. 2018. Black Cumin Seed Oil: Top Benefits, Uses, & Side Effects. [Online]. [11 February 2020]. Available from: https://globalhealing.com/natural-health/black-cumin-seed-oil/

[3] Toro, R. 2013. Live Science Diagram of the human immune system. [Online]. [11 April 2020]. Available from: https://www.livescience.com/38028-how-the-human-body-s-immune-system-works-infographic.html

[4] Servan-Schreiber, D (2008). Anticancer A New Way of Life: Penguin Group.

[5] Fraser, C. 2018. Study: Vegan Diet and Lifestyle

Changes Causes More Than 500 Genes to Change in 3 Months. [Online]. [19 April 2020]. Available from: https://livelovefruit.com/vegan-diet-changes-500-genes-three-months/

[6] Fraser, C. 2018. Milk and Mucus: Why Dairy is The Major Cause of Your Phlegm, Mucus and Congestion Issues. [Online]. [20 February 2020]. Available from: https://livelovefruit.com/milk-and-mucus-production/

[7] Dr Brown, S.E & Trivieri, L (2013). The Acid Alkaline Food Guide. (2nd ed.): Square One.

[8] Young. 2012. DR OTTO HEINRICH WARBURG ON THE ROOT CAUSE OF CANCER. [Online]. [17 March 2020]. Available from: https://phoreveryoung.wordpress.com/2012/02/20/dr-otto-heinrich-warburg-on-the-root-cause-of-cancer/

[9] Wim Hof. c2020. Welcome to the Official Wim Hof Method Website. [Online]. [17 March 2020]. Available from: https://www.wimhofmethod.com/

[10] Julie, K. c2019. What Happens to Your Body When You Start Eating Cleaner? [Online]. [30 March 2020]. Available from: https://thehealthyfish.com/happens-body-start-eating-cleaner/

[11] Dr Murray, M, Dr Pizzorno, J & Pizzorno, L (2005). The Encyclopedia Of Healing Foods. (1 ed.): Atria Books.

[12] Elliott, B. 2018. 8 Great Reasons to Include Chickpeas in Your Diet. [Online]. [25 March 2020]. Available from: https://www.healthline.com/nutrition/chickpeas-nutrition-benefits

[13] Duelli, N. 2008. Spirulina & Chlorella Nature's super algae. [Online]. [04 April 2020]. Available from: https://www.alive.com/health/spirulina-chlorella/

[14] Dr Fife, B (2008). Coconut Water for Health and Healing: Piccadilly Books.

[15] Karohs, E (2016). Marijuana Killed My Cancer and is keeping me cancer free: Step-by-step guide how to kill your cancer with cannabis The healing miracle of CBD plus THC: CreateSpace Independent Publishing Platform.

[16] Levy, J. 2019. Is Coconut Sugar Good for You? [Online]. [04 April 2020]. Available from: https://draxe.com/nutrition/coconut-sugar/

[17] Cancer research UK. 2019. Cancer risk statistics. [Online]. [28 April 2020]. Available from: https://www.cancerresearchuk.org/health-professional/cancer-statistics/risk

[18] Pappas, S. 2010. Optimism Boosts Immune System. [Online]. [20 April 2020]. Available from: https://www.livescience.com/8158-optimism-boosts-immune-system.html

[19] Simpson, R. c2014. Rick Simpson. [On-

line]. [22 March 2020]. Available from: http://phoenixtears.ca/

[20] Harrigan, C. 2017. Healing Cancer with Cannabis: The Rick Simpson Story - YouTube. [Online]. [22 March 2020]. Available from: https://www.youtube.com/watch?time_continue=17&v=Ak3Zo7-hNO0&feature=emb_logo

[21] Dr Dispenza, J. 2019. Opening the door to the supernatural. Becoming Supernatural: How Common People Are Doing the Uncommon: Hay House Inc, pp.

[22] Hay, L (1984). You Can Heal Your Life. (2nd ed.): Hay House Inc.

[23] Emily's quotes. c2020. Emily's quotes. [Online]. [04 May 2020]. Available from: https://emilysquotes.com/the-cells-in-your-body-react-to-everything-that-your-mind-says-negativity-brings-down-your-immune-system/

[24] Juliana. c2017. The Curious Butterfly. [Online]. [04 May 2020]. Available from: https://www.curiousbutterfly.org/7-mindfulness-quotes/

[25] Goodreads. c2020. Joe Dispenza Quotes. [Online]. [04 May 2020]. Available from: https://www.goodreads.com/work/quotes/18108532-breaking-the-habit-of-being-yourself-how-to-lose-your-mind-and-create-a

[26] Body&soul reconnection. c2020. YOUR POWER TO CREATE A PLACEBO OR NO-CEBO EFFECT. [Online]. [05 May 2020]. Available from: https://bodyandsoulreconnection.com/your-power-to-create-a-placebo-or-nocebo-effect/

[27] Catherine. c2019. How The Body Regenerates Itself. [Online]. [05 May 2020]. Available from: https://foodsthathealyou.com/how-the-body-regenerates-itself/

[28] Bosh. c2018. Bosh! [Online]. [09 May 2020]. Available from: https://www.bosh.tv/

[29] Cultivating kindness. 2018. How to Re-wire Your Brain to Be Happy. [Online]. [12 April 2020]. Available from: https://cultivating-kindness.com/2018/01/25/how-to-rewire-your-brain-to-be-happy/

[30] Emily's quotes. c2020. Emily's quotes. [Online]. [05 May 2020]. Available from: https://emilysquotes.com/your-mind-will-always-believe-everything-you-tell-it-feed-it-faith/

[31] Hay, L. 1984. The List. You Can Heal Your Life: Hay House Inc, pp.

[32] Hicks, E.&. J. 2004. The Different Degrees of Your Emotional Guidance Scale. In: Kramer ed. Ask and It Is Given: Learning to Manifest Your Desires: Hay House Inc, pp.

[33] Emily's quotes. c2020. Emily's

quotes. [Online]. [05 May 2020]. Available from: https://emilysquotes.com/ we-are-here-to-change-the-world-not-just-follow-rules-earn-money-and-die/

[34] Goodreads. c2020. A New Earth Quotes By Eckhart Tolle. [Online]. [04 May 2020]. Available from: https://www.goodreads.com/work/ quotes/2567181-a-new-earth-awakening-to-your-life-s-purpose

[35] Naturalknow. 2020. Dr Sebi mucous is the cause of every disease, best ways to get rid of phlegm after eating and clear mucus from your throat. [Online]. [28 January 2021]. Available from: https://natural-know.com/dr-sebi-mucous-is-the-cause-of-every-disease-best-ways-to-get-rid-of-phlegm-after-eating-and-clear-mucus-from-your-throat/

[36] Universoul awakening. 2020. 288 Eckhart Tolle Quotes. [Online]. [1 March 2021]. Available from: https://www.universoulawakening.com/365-eckhart-tolle-quotes/

[37] Az quotes. 2021. Rudolf Steiner quote: For every human illness, somewhere. [Online]. [21 February 2021]. Available from: https://www.az-quotes.com/quote/874272

[38] Livelovefruit. 2018. 15 Best Natural Antibiotics and Antibacterials That Should Be in Every Home. [Online]. [16 February 2021]. Available from: https://livelovefruit.com/best-natural-antibiotics/

[39] Great awakening report. 2019. DOCUMENTARY: THE GROUNDED WALKING BAREFOOT. [Online]. [21 February 2021]. Available from: https://greatawakeningreport.com/documentary-the-grounded-walking-barefoot/

[40] Cbdlifeuk. 205-2020. Study confirms cannabinoids occur naturally in human breast milk. [Online]. [1 March 2021]. Available from: https://cbdlifeuk.com/study-confirms-cannabinoids-occur-naturally-human-breast-milk/

[41] Emily's quotes. c2020. The moment you start acting like life is a blessing, it will start to feel like one. [Online]. [2 March 2021]. Available from: https://emilysquotes.com/the-moment-you-start-acting-like-life-is-a-blessing-it-will-start-to-feel-like-one/

[42] Grass root level. 2018. Why Cow Milk is NOT MEANT FOR HUMAN?. [Online]. [09 March 2021]. Available from: https://grassrootlevel.home.blog/2018/12/27/why-cow-milk-is-not-meant-for-

human/

[43] Northwestern medicine. c2021. Dairy: Do You Really Need It?. [Online]. [10 March 2021]. Available from: https://www.nm.org/healthbeat/healthy-tips/nutrition/dairy-do-you-really-need-it

[44] Healthline. 2019. Natural Ways to Reduce Uric Acid in the Body. [Online]. [10 March 2021]. Available from: https://www.healthline.com/health/how-to-reduce-uric-acid

[45] Brainyquote. c2021. Acceptance quotes-Brainyquote. [Online]. [11 March 2021]. Available from: https://www.brainyquote.com/topics/acceptance-quotes

[46] Goodreads. c2021. Lauren Jauregui quotes. [Online]. [12 March 2021]. Available from: https://www.goodreads.com/author/quotes/16366094.Lauren_Jauregui

Printed in Great Britain
by Amazon

59757793R00063